Weight Loss for the *Mind*

Stuart Wilde

Hay House, Inc.
Carson, CA

BOOKS BY STUART WILDE:

Miracles

Affirmations

The Quickening

The Force

Life Was Never Meant to Be a Struggle

The Trick to Money Is Having Some

The Secrets of Life

Whispering Winds of Change

Contents

1

Opinion and Feeling

Chapter One

As you walk down a city street and look at reality, all the things you see—buildings, houses, cars—are, in fact, an external manifestation of someone's opinion. A building is placed where it is, shaped as it is, because someone had the opinion to construct it that way and to place it on a particular spot.

Internal reality—our perception of life, the psychology and metaphysics of our humanity—is constructed in the same way. It is formed solely by opinion. We perceive what we believe.

We mostly inherit our broad-based opinions and feelings from others, or construct them from common experiences. They make us predictable. They form and define our reality. Those opinions are as real and as solid as the gas station on the corner.

In this booklet, *Weight Loss for the Mind,* we look at the opinions prevalent in our mass psychology and how many of them cause us anguish. With a few simple flips of the mind, and a little psychological and spiritual understanding, you can release ninety-five percent of all anguish. The other five percent you'll probably hang onto for the moment, out of habit.

But you'll gradually dismiss the last five percent and free yourself from the opinions you've acquired from others as well as those you have established yourself. This will liberate you from the collective emotion and the anguish it offers. Serenity flows naturally from a heightened perception. You process and understand things differently.

If you like your spiritual growth, your psychological integration and personal healing on the hurry up, as I do, this little book is for you.

Weight is described as the gravity exerted when a particular mass comes into close proximity with another. Your physical weight is established by the mass of the earth. If you are overweight it may not be your fault at all, it could be that the planet is out of balance and it is exerting a bit too much gravity upon you!

Scientists can't tell us exactly what gravity is. They postulate that it is caused by minute particles called gravitons. As yet, we can't find gravitons so we don't know for certain. But we *can* observe what gravity does.

Gravity is, in fact, the expression of a contradiction. A large mass like our planet contradicts a smaller mass like your body, forcing it to remain within the planet's gravitational influence.

It's interesting that in English we use the same word for the force of gravity and for seriousness. When we say that something is grave, we mean it impacts our emotions and affects us negatively. We feel the presence of a psychological mass exerting itself upon us. Negative emotion and the force of gravity are really two manifestations of the same force.

The mental and emotional weight you experience as stress, or anguish, is exactly like the force of gravity. It relies on two or more psychological masses in your mind to establish a contradictory relationship with each other. Your reactions to the day-to-day circumstances of life form one mass in your mind, and the ideas that exist around your opinion form the other mass. Across these two masses flows a psychological tension which generates an emotional reaction.

For life's circumstances to generate negative emotion they have to contradict your opinion. If circumstances don't contradict one of your opinions, your reaction is neutral. When circumstances enhance your opinions, they generate positive emotion for you.

So negative emotion (psychological weight) is only possible when there exists in your mind two opposing mental forces. Imagine them as two large rocks. One is constructed from loosely interconnected ideas, which are grouped initially in your mind by their similarity. They are held together and made solid by personal argument, and form your opinion—your expectations. The other rock is created by your reaction to and perception of life's circumstances. It often stands juxtaposed to the first mass, contradicting it.

Negative emotion, therefore, is nothing more than the experience of being contradicted. You have certain opinions and expectations; and life comes along and contradicts those opinions, thus generating negative emotion.

WEIGHT LOSS FOR THE MIND

How do these expectations and opinions arise?

Just as a rock is made up of a series of atoms that give it mass, when your thoughts and ideas are grouped around a personal issue they gradually generate a psychological mass in your mind.

For such a mass to exert power over you, there has to be an underlying opinion to bind the whole thing together. That opinion usually flows from some personal need you think is important.

Opinion is like the nucleus of an atom— it is a *mental* power source. Your ideas hover around it, like the subatomic particles that circle a nucleus. As they orbit your opinion, the personal arguments they give out back it up. When enough similar ideas gather to form a solid opinion, they establish a psychological mass in your mind. That mass is extremely solid and difficult to shift.

The human personality relies on these psychological masses to grant it solidity. It's vital for your personality to feel that it is correct and just, and that the ideas it holds are holy and good and, above all, right. People with crazy and irrational ideas often go to great lengths to justify them.

From the psychological mass created by your opinions flows the view you take on a particular issue. From that impression flow feelings which we call emotion.

The crux of all anguish lies in this issue of opinion and contradiction. Once you get it, and see how it affects your life and your well-being, you can free yourself for ever.

If you want a powerful, joyous existence, get a grip on the issue of contradiction - and you are free.

Realization

If your personality were programed to accept contradictions as natural, and if it did not react, you could not experience negative emotion or anguish.

2

Contradiction and Expectancy

Chapter Two

It's a three-fold gain when you understand how these contradictions of life affect you. First, you can eliminate some of them immediately. Second, you can design your life to avoid most of them. Third, you can develop tools that allow you to accept, unemotionally, those contradictions you can't avoid.

Doing these three things, you return to your natural god-like state, serene, happy, and entertained by the wonder and grace of this strange gift we call life.

How do these contradictions arise?

Most of them are just inherent to our programing. The human personality exists in strange cyber space, hovering above the ground at five to six feet or slightly more, trapped in nowhere land, some place in the brain.

Strange isn't it? We all think we're here. In fact we are a hovercraft with no landing gear! The human personality never actually lands on earth. Even if you stand on your head, your personality is still somewhere beyond the thickness of your skull above the ground. That sets up an uncomfortable contradiction.

Your personality has to use the body as its link between the infinite cyber space in which it dwells, and the earthly dimension from which its experiences flow.

The body is finite. Death is the ultimate contradiction. It is natural, therefore, that most people feel a bit insecure.

Life, for many, is a futile attempt to become secure in a dimension that is intrinsically insecure. People constantly fight that, rather than accept the strangeness of the human lesson as a beautiful thing. God must have a marvelous sense of humor—the contradictions of life are awesome and funny and very appealing. I find them heroic.

- *We have to embrace infinity inside a mortal body.*

- *We have to believe in a god we can't see.*

- *We have to learn to love in a dimension where there is so much hatred.*

- *We have to see abundance when people constantly talk of shortages and lack.*

- *We have to discover freedom where control is the state religion.*

- *We have to develop self-worth while people criticize and belittle us.*

- *We have to see beauty where there is ugliness.*

- *We have to embrace kindness and positive attitudes when surrounded by uncertainty.*

- *We have to feel safe in spite of our concerns.*

Yes, the heroism of our condition is most endearing.

Transcendence is nothing more than learning to accept the contradictions of life without resistance.

Embracing these contradictions is not natural to us. In fact we are taught as children to resist. So, for example, as a small child you were programed to believe that being wet and cold was a negative experience. If your mother ever left you standing in the rain, you probably reacted emotionally and cried. Now, as an adult, you may have the same programed negative reaction to getting wet. Around it hover all the variables: rain ruins your clothes and messes with your hair, rain is uncomfortable as it runs down your neck, rain is cold, cold makes you sick, and so on.

So one mass of energy in your mind says, we have to be cozy, warm and comfortable, to feel positive, happy and secure. Then along comes the rain. Now it's belting down and you're miles from shelter. Suddenly circumstances—the cold wet conditions—contradict your opinion or desire.

Now two masses have established a relationship in your mind, each pulling on the other. Negative emotion flows from the contradiction generated by the cold rain. But is it the rain that is negative? Or is it just your reaction to the rain that causes the contradiction? Water falling from above has no intrinsic quality—positive or negative. When you took a shower this morning you weren't moaning and groaning.

`Ah! But that was hot water.'

`So, it's the temperature of the water that's bothering you is it?'

`Precisely.'

But what if you just accept cold water as a part of life? Sometimes it rains. You can get angry and resist, or you can relax and just 'do' rain. The circumstances haven't changed—your reaction has. As soon as you agree to 'do' rain and stop resisting, the rain becomes warmer and gradually more comfortable. Eventually, you can 'do' rain indefinitely and even enjoy it.

If you have never 'done' rain, try this: put out your finest clothes, including your most expensive shoes, and wait. When it starts to rain, dress up and step out, walking steadily, head held high. Don't bat an eyelid. Have no opinion, keep walking, love the rain, accept it, make it your friend.

Eventually your resistance falls to zero. The rain disappears, in your mind anyway. While you are 'doing' rain, you can amuse yourself by watching others 'not doing' rain properly. There's a bit of fun in that.

If you can't bring yourself to 'do' rain immediately, at least regularly make the ego do things that contradict it. Start small. Take cold showers. Give away your over-coat, wear fewer clothes.

Stop talking about the weather altogether. Don't comment on conditions, just experience them. After all, when people say it's cold, what do they mean? They mean it is colder than their expectation. In effect, there is no hot and cold, only temperature that rises and falls sometimes.

All of life's circumstances, like the rain, are neutral. Life has no particular quality, positive or negative, other than the labels we give it. Never forget that.

Even death is neutral. We have no way of knowing how we might react to death. Perhaps life is really crummy compared to death. The hand-wringing and anguish we suffer is probably all for nothing. I have a sneaky suspicion that graduating from the earth plane may be one heck of a celebration.

It's the programed expectancy that stuffs us up and causes us pain. Not the circumstances.

Expectancy sets up the possibility of contradictions.

Yes, we expect the best, but we must learn not to react when we don't get what we want. If you are diligent, and you concentrate and take right action, you'll most likely always get the best result. But you must love life and accept it when it doesn't go your way.

Be heroic, become a warrior. When faced with an adverse situation, don't react, just accept it. Act calmly. Act powerfully. If you don't know what to do immediately, do nothing—wait until the answer comes to you.

Be mature and take the emotion out of situations. Act in the strongest way possible, given the situation. You can easily train your personality to 'do' life rather than fight it. Don't be a self-indulgent wimp. Sometimes life isn't cozy, safe or guaranteed. If you're up to your eyes in muck and bullets, first 'do' bullets then 'do' muck.

It's so simple. It's our silly expectancy and the ego's self-importance that demands things have to be one way or the other. That's what causes us all the pain—not life itself.

Life is mostly guesswork. You will usually guess more or less right, and sometimes you'll guess wrong. When you guess wrong, don't react—love your mistakes, and don't beat yourself up.

Hey! You thought you had enough gas in the car and you didn't, so now you're 'doing' walking. So what.

Just walk.

Realization

*The circumstances of life have no
particular quality, either positive or
negative. They are neutral. Don't resist
them, even the ones that scare you silly.
When faced with adversity,
buy the solution—not the emotion.
Teach that to others.*

3

Emotion and Desire

Chapter Three

When ideas come together in your mind to form an opinion, and when that opinion is seen by you to be pleasing, the personality backs up that opinion by investing it with emotion.

Using emotion, the ego can take an idea (opinion) and make it special, more real and more important.

Emotion is the tool the personality uses to grant its opinions credibility and value. It's how the personality feels worthwhile. It is also how the personality gets what it

27

wants. It can wield emotion like a baseball bat, manipulating others to react to its needs and desires.

We learn the trick as children. A bit of theatrics, temper tantrums—howling at 120 decibels in the middle of the supermarket—worked marvellously when we wanted an ice cream. Emotion was how we got grown-ups to take notice.

The more insignificant a person feels, the more they will seek to bolster their vulnerability by using emotion. They will bathe in it, constantly talking about their emotions, making them special and elevating them to a grand scale. They will also be fascinated by the emotions of others, fueling their need, constantly discussing emotional issues, watching emotional TV shows. Living in the emotion of local and world events, along with the momentary reactions they have to their own lives. The process makes them feel better temporarily.

However, there are several downsides to the use of emotion in this way. Let's say you watch a news story on TV about a war, and you buy into the emotion of it all. Even though your conscious mind knows you are not involved, a subconscious pollution is taking place that makes you feel less safe and more vulnerable. Watching others reacting to situations that are out of control reminds you of the possibility of your own collapse.

Further, the more you allow yourself to be imbalanced emotionally in your own issues, the greater the ego content. Once the personality has a large part of itself invested emotionally in an issue, any contradiction of its position is seen as a great personal trauma or threat.

Emotion elevates the issues of the ego to a greater importance. It grants the ego power. Other people react to our emotion, especially negative emotion. The ego believes that if it is considered important by others, that will make it more special, less vulnerable, and therefore safer. The more power the ego can garner, the more people will observe it to be different, elevated, above the herd, divine—and beyond the central issue of man, which is death. Sometimes, the use of emotion is nothing more than the personality seeking to avoid what it sees as death by insignificance.

In using emotion initially to help us feel more secure, we actually set ourselves up to experience a greater insecurity and personal affront when things go the wrong way.

Through experiencing life, you gradually form habits and establish preferences from which you develop hopes and expectancy. A hope or expectancy is, in fact, an opinion; when you lace opinion with emotion you generate desire. When life contradicts your deep-rooted emotional desires, you tend to take it more personally than when a hope is denied.

Here's how the process works in practice. You'll start with a vague hope such as, `I'd like a day off work'. Around that will float ideas that back up that hope. `I'm entitled to a day off, I've worked hard.' Now the personality selects from its memory and reasoning arguments to justify its opinion and make the idea right. However, the hope still has no real weight—it is still in the process of developing mass via personal argument and inner dialogue.

So to give the idea real importance, your personality will begin to invest itself in the idea by lacing it with emotion. The `day off' issue starts to become a vital part of the personality's affirmation of self. `I need a day off. I'm desperate for a day off. Life owes me a day off. Other people have time off. I'm a good person, an important person, my health will suffer if I don't have a day off. Taking the day off is right and proper and just.' And so on...

Let's say the reality is that you have loads of obligations, and circumstances won't allow you the luxury of a day off.

At this point the ego flares up, taking the issue very personally. It will see denial as a personal affront and an assault on its integrity and stability. This will begin to erode the ego's sense of security. The unfulfilled desire becomes an affirmation of the personality's powerlessness. The ultimate powerlessness for the personality is death. So the 'day off work' now subconsciously becomes an issue of life and death.

The personality begins to resonate weakness through its insecurity, and its psychological and metaphysical strength breaks down quite quickly. From life's rich tapestry flow circumstances that confirm and sustain that self-perceived weakness.

The physical body reacts to the overall message of weakness and now you have the makings of a rotten little head cold. The car won't start. Your boss loads you with even more work; a bill you can't pay plops through the mail box. Now you can really feel victimized. A hundred insecurities are triggered in your mind. The natural reaction is to feel threatened. Anger develops. Culprits have to be found. Someone must be doing it to you. Interpersonal wars develop. It's a zoo!

The emotion and weight of it all may lie with you for days or even longer—until the personality experiences a major win or uplift that will allow it to get on top of the situation, and so feel secure and worthwhile and happy. All this performance can be traced back to the thought you had last Thursday which said, 'I'd love a day off work.'

It's wonderful how this system works. We start with a vague idea; we back that with reasoning to confirm the idea to ourselves. Then we lace it with emotion, investing ourselves in it. Then we go through a ludicrous emotional power-play, laying our life on the line, in an attempt to get what we want. When circumstances call our bluff, we're devastated.

If the emotional content you lace into an idea is sustained over a period of time, and if your desire is continually denied, it can lead to yearning. In metaphysical terms, yearning is the act of leaning toward or leaning over an idea, a hope perhaps.

As I have said in my other books, in leaning emotionally toward your dreams, you actually push them away. The emotion of your desire creates a metaphysical gap between you and the condition or scenario you desire, making it harder for you to pull that desired condition to you. The gap is established because yearning is a powerful affirmation which categorically states, `I do not have the thing I yearn for.'

In constantly affirming that you haven't got what you want, you deteriorate and disempower what you do have. More important, you pattern your subtle metaphysical energy with an overlay, like a thumbprint, that is discordant with the very thing you do want.

There is one further consideration: the thing you desire— fame, success, money, opportunity, romance, whatever—will usually come to you, in part, through the actions of others. It's your fellow humans who help carry your desires from the nebulous metaphysics of possibility to your immediate reality, where you get to feast upon your dreams.

In yearning, we become self-indulgent. Self-indulgence bothers people. They sense it and feel put upon. They don't like the added burden of your emotional weight impinging upon them. It reminds them of the times they needed things and were denied. They react by feeling themselves the underdog, victimized by your indulgence. They will deny you, hoping to control you or have power over you. In doing so, they hope to drop you from what they see as your unreasonable, superior stance.

Further, pining and yearning can become obsessive. Obsession is a serious disease of the ego—it creates emotional weight, blinding you to opportunities that do exist. It also makes you apathetic. By constantly affirming that you haven't got what you need, the body begins to believe it doesn't have what *it* needs. That makes it weaker. In the act of perpetually yearning, the ego eventually finds itself in a stagnant void, the lack of energy gradually eats the body.

If the condition persists, it will eventually kill you.

Don't yearn, act. Take fifteen minutes of each day to visualize, as though granted, the condition or circumstance you want. Create a mental setting, see yourself with the object of your desire. Become a part of it, let it become a part of you. Allow it to *be* you. Then rise, head out, and do something that moves you toward your dream—something powerful and positive.

Remember, you have to travel toward your dream. It is very unlikely that, unaided, your dream will find you. It's not impossible, but you might be a long time waiting, maybe forever.

By the way, if you want to increase the intensity of your visualizations and meditations, read the chapter on *Turbo-Thought* in my book, *The Quickening*. In it, I discuss how to use the sexual heat of Kundalini to lace your visions with a metaphysical power that is close to unstoppable.

Please note—if the object of your desire is that another person should act in a certain way, put that out and visualize it—but remember they have their own destiny pattern, and it may not coincide with your desire for them.

If you could hope and dream and want things without wrapping those ideas with emotion, you'd be a very happy person. You wouldn't react if life makes you wait or if life denies you completely. You'd be perfectly at one and balanced all the time. It's the emotion you invest that makes you sad and sets up contradictions. The less you put yourself on the line emotionally, the less pain you suffer.

Realization

Don't use emotion as a self-indulgent tool to attract attention or to make yourself and your ideas important. Instead, act powerfully and concisely. Be active. Create energy, give of yourself. Let others need you, rather than you needing them and acting to win their approval.

4

Eliminating Fear
Through Perception

Chapter Four

The greatest cause of anguish is fear. Your first step in conquering fear is to learn not to be frightened of fear itself. Start by seeing fear as your friend, not your tormentor. It's OK to be scared at times. In fact, fear keeps you safe. It heightens your perception and allows you to take corrective action when needed. All fear stems initially from the fear of death.

It's the death of *things* that scares us. Not just physical death, but the termination of familiar things—the end of a relationship, a job, a habit. Sometimes it's a

43

rhythm that is about to change, or your location, or a feeling of certainty you've clung to.

It's *change* we resist. Yet change is the spiritual universe's way of keeping you alive and fresh. We live in a rapidly developing world. If you're not changing, life is leaving you behind. Things will get tougher, not easier.

Once you can accept change and endings, and not see them as personal affronts, most of the fear will dissipate. By attempting to hang onto circumstances and conditions whose energy is spent, you strain yourself.

Constantly remind yourself of what you already know. Nothing is guaranteed or certain. It doesn't have to be.

You can be balanced in all circumstances.

Fear of change and fear of the unknown are just malaise of the ego. You don't have to know what will happen in the future in order to feel safe. In fact, the more you evolve and expand your consciousness, the more unpredictable life becomes. The less certain you are, the higher you have climbed.

Cozy, unchanging rhythms are manifestations of the intellect. Often dull and stifling, they are only suited to the lazy or those who lack courage—those who prefer to exist in a confined, defendable area where nothing unexpected can happen. Important fish in little puddles, swimming in their own effluent.

You don't need a puddle, and there's not much oxygen in a pond either. Pick a river. Flow and go. Be fearless, believe. Let the energy of life carry you spontaneously from stepping stone to stepping stone. Win your freedom. Reach for the open sea. All will be well.

Resistance to change is mostly ego.

If your ego is frightened, ridicule it. Or just chat to it and tell it everything's fine. Then step to your spiritual side. Embrace the spirit, as it has embraced you from the beginning of time, in the warm glow of its celestial light. That's the heroic way.

Realization

All fear is nothing more than the ego's expectancy of an upcoming contradiction. Most of it is not real. Dissipate its power by refusing to buy the emotion. Make fear your friend. Talk to it. Accommodate it as a helper and ally and most of your fear will change or disappear completely.

5

Healing Confusion

Chapter Five

In our vain attempt to achieve security, we do a lot of thinking. We're constantly trying to guess what's going to happen next.

Modern life is full of choices. Given that many things are unpredictable, making the right choice is sometimes a difficult process. Confusion is endemic to the Western tribes. Millions of human hours are given to the process.

Confusion is a mind game that clouds your inner knowing and causes you to

WEIGHT LOSS FOR THE MIND

vacillate. It makes for indecisive action, poor reasoning, and instability—which manifest as erratic behavior and stress. When you are uncommitted and confused, your results are poor or you fail completely.

Would you like to eliminate confusion from your life for ever?

Yes or no?

If your answer is `no' please skip this bit. If your answer is `yes' please read on.

Confusion comes, first and foremost, from questions. You can't be confused unless you first ask a question. If you are serious about eliminating confusion, begin by reducing the number of questions you ask yourself.

Yes, you can ponder about your life. And yes, meditate and feel things through. But it's the diarrhea of questions you ask yourself that drives you nuts.

Do this: agree from this day forth to eliminate ninety percent of all your questions. Next, agree never to make any decisions solely via logic and intellect. Use your feelings, even though they may seem illogical at times. Given two or three alternatives, you are either going to *know* through your feelings what direction to take, or you'll be unsure.

If you know, go.

If you don't know, and you have to mentally grind the options back and forth for days on end, none of the possibilities offered can be right at this time anyway.

They may never be right. Decision should be natural and come from the heart. If it doesn't feel right and you are not sure, do nothing.

Watching and waiting is my way. However, if you have to approach things intellectually because that is your habit, then, rather than pondering and being confused, collect information. Most people who make intellectual and logical decisions suffer hits because of a lack of information. Never advance your troops into a valley without sending a few scouts up to the high ground. You don't want to plow into situations outnumbered, disadvantaged, and unsure.

In passing, here are a few ideas about conflicts—which, after all, are a major source of mental weight. My preferred method is to avoid them, by watching everything, all of the time, and taking early corrective action. Or, by not giving away control in the first place—which is how most of the trouble arises. Almost always, conflicts are various forms of ego-related turf wars.

My next move is to always try to walk away before the conflict gets going, and to agree to release whatever the conflict is about.

My third recommendation deals only with situations where the conflict really is unavoidable. First, evaluate your chances of success. Never go into situations where winning is in doubt. If you know you're bound to win, start by pretending to retreat, and get the emotion out of the situation. Your feigned retreat puts others off their guard.

Then, quietly garner all your strength. When you're ready—and not before—come at the conflict with the element of surprise, and with the full force of your power and concentration. All guns blazing. Never use a sledgehammer to crack a nut if you can use a ten-ton pile driver. Victories should be swift, bloodless and completed in the most efficient manner possible.

Try also to offer the opposition an honorable surrender. That's the kindest way. It's gracious and spiritual to allow their ego an intellectual escape route even if it is mostly hooey. You don't want to destroy people. The object of this journey is to expand goodness. You are not here to judge and punish others.

In relation to confusion, remember this: everything gives off energy. When your feelings can't read a situation properly, that tells you the circumstances you're considering lack energy. Either the situation is wrong for you, or you are not ready, or this is not the proper time.

What you choose to do in life is not usually as important as the level of power and concentration you bring to your action, and the timing you choose when exerting that power. Timing and concerted action are the keys to success. Selecting direction is tertiary to timing and power.

In helping others resolve their confusion, never ask the individual what they think, always ask how they *feel* about an issue. Then ask them what they want. Help them discover whether they really want what it is they think they want. As I said, most wanting is ego.

Then get them to look at whether their want is reasonable, given their energy and circumstances. And, finally, is it likely? Most individuals are professional dreamers who, in fact, only need the dreaming—they don't need the responsibility or the action required to materialize their dreams.

When a dream becomes a reality, the experience of it naturally changes. Usually, reality is a letdown compared to the vision. The idea of their dream actually becoming a part of their lives is often too daunting. So, many ensure they are never disappointed, by underperforming, or selecting actions that ensure their dream remains just that, only a dream.

Realization

*Confusion is a manifestation of an
unsettled intellect. The intellect is
dominated by the ego. So confusion is
mostly the ego's chatter harassing your life.
Train the ego to ask fewer questions and
answer most of the others with,
"I don't know and I don't care."*

6

Healing Frustration

Chapter Six

$\mathcal{F}$rustration comes from expectancy, the emotional outcropping of which is desire. We use past rhythms and experiences, hoping to extrapolate from that the timing of some future event. Sometimes that works and often it doesn't. Most frustration stems from slotting hopes and plans into preselected time frames which you consider necessary to your happiness and well-being. That's not a mature way to conduct your life.

You know things usually take longer than you think they will, because it's easier to think something through than it is to carry it out in practice. Important things always take longer than you expect. That's because they are usually more complex, and because often the circumstance or condition you desire eludes you until you have matured and grown to where you can not only handle it, but claim it.

The other main cause of frustration is people. We usually try to slot people into patterns that suit us. That is a futile exercise in self-destruction. You can certainly encourage people and hope they might change, but in the end you either love them unconditionally for what they are or you have to agree to walk.

In my early twenties I owned a clothing company. We hired a great designer who was the mainstay of the corporation. She was indispensable. Exercising power over us, she totally controlled the fate of the company—and she knew it. After a while her ego kicked in with a vengeance and she became temperamental, capricious and unreliable. As she wobbled, the whole company wobbled with her. She caused endless trouble because we had no real control.

From that day forth I decided I would never suffer the same situation again. Now, everyone in my life is dispensable. I hold no permanent emotion to any situation or person—including family and friends. Everything can be released. Nothing is obligatory. When people know that is your attitude, they tend to be more equitable and realistic. They certainly are more caring, more diligent.

You can work with people, and you can be loving and patient while they grow and respond to positive input. But in the end, if they won't change or—in the case of an employee—toe the line and support the cause, then you have to let them go. Never get into a situation where someone is so indispensable you can't get rid of them.

This is especially true of romance, where one tends to give away control more easily. Nobody should ever be essential to you. Falling in love is fun, but don't let it blind you to the fact that there are five billion characters out there to bat at. Make sure the focus of your affection is constantly reminded that he or she isn't too vital and that, though you may love them and you may have chosen them, you are also aware of the vast field of opportunity lying just beyond the front door.

It's fine to rely on people if you are really sure of the person you are relying on. But most individuals aren't too solid, especially under pressure. If you have to rely on people, be sure you spread the risk. No one person should hold the key to your life. It always amazes me how people will entrust their entire life's savings to some character or organization they hardly know. Take many small, calculated risks rather than plunge all of yourself on the one bet.

A mistake we frequently make when dealing with people is to expect them to remain the same. We remember them as they used to be. In fact people change, minute by minute, second by second. They suffer mood swings, energy shifts, emotional waves and psychological changes. That often makes them unpredictable, erratic and irresponsible. In many cases, relying on others means giving away your power. Sometimes you have little or no choice. However, you should design your life to avoid it as much as possible.

The other source of frustration for many is the experience of not getting what they want. The solution to that is to not want whatever it is you think you want. If you can't manage that, at least want less things. The more things you have to have, the more vulnerable you become. If you are mature and evolved, you'll need nothing from anyone—and what little you do need you can provide for yourself.

Remember, most of the things you think you need are ego trips designed to bolster your image and your perception of security. Many of them are not particularity vital. You'll waste a lot of energy satisfying your ego only to find that, as soon as it's got what it wants, it ignores all your efforts and promptly nails another list of demands to your forehead.

The ego will always try to force you to slave for its vision. I wouldn't stand for that *BS* if I were you.

Realization

Frustration stems from the nasty habit of allowing the ego to decide the timing and delivery of its desires. If you blindfold the ego with discipline and never show it the menu of life, it doesn't bitch about the food—it's thrilled that you are eating to keep it alive.

7

Healing Guilt

Chapter Seven

Guilt is silly, self-indulgent and weak. It's often an emotional outcropping of a poor self-image.

You didn't come to earth because you are perfect—quite the reverse. You came because you needed to learn lessons that are available here. If you've stuffed up some aspect of your life, all it means is that you attended the seminar of life and got the message.

There is no real sin—only high energy and low energy. If your actions were less than best, you can forgive yourself and resolve to do better next time. Probably there won't be a next time. You usually only have to stuff up once to get the point. Certainly you might have acted better, but you didn't. Forgive yourself. You're not a bloody angel. If you were, you wouldn't be here.

The past is past and can't be fixed. The only tragedy is when you carry a negative memory of it into the future. Absolve yourself. If needs be, create a solemn ceremony, light a candle, say a prayer or meditate, release yourself from previous stuff-ups. If you've hurt people in some way, write them a mental letter and mail it to their heart—tell them you're sorry. Or, better still, pop round and apologize to them personally. That's very cathartic for them and for you.

Don't forget, the way people perceive you is clouded by their own program and by what is often an extreme lack of perception. They see you in whatever terms benefit and confirm their opinion. How you *actually* are is mostly a secret. It lies deep within your spiritual self and often is not seen by others. Cling to that reality, and never mind what people think. Trying to win the approval of others by doing a goody-goody routine is often just a carry-over from the child within that seeks parental acceptance. It's not necessary for a mature adult.

Worrying about what people think disempowers your values. It places control in *their* opinions and *their* reactions.

Let people think what they like. They will anyway. You don't have to be a politician and act just to win favor. Instead, act as honorably and correctly as possible. Either people will approve or they won't. Leave it up to them, and remember not to ask them. That way you won't have to stuff around finding out what they think of you, processing their reactions, and explaining yourself to them. That's energy down the drain. Don't mess with it.

Finally, guilt is one of the emotional cudgels people use to establish control, especially in family situations. Don't use guilt to control others and never succumb to the ploy yourself. Call it as you see it. When others see that you won't play ball, they'll back off. Once they hook you emotionally, via guilt, it's hard to break free. Any escape you do engineer will usually involve a big fight. The trick is to politely and lovingly sidestep their emotional net before it ensnares you.

Realization

*To pine for an alternative past is a
waste of energy. In the pristine
world of your infinite spiritual self
there is no sin or negative
energy. There is only compassion, learning
and unconditional love and forgiveness.
Remind yourself and those around you of
this fact. In the light of God everything
is healed and seen to be perfect.*

8

Healing Anger

Chapter Eight

You can't develop a lightness of being without sooner or later healing your anger. So let's get rid of that, pronto!

As I said in my book, *Whispering Winds of Change,* all anger comes initially from an impending sense of loss or an actual loss.

When the ego has a part of its importance invested in material things, it will take the disappearance of those items as an affront. So, when the stereo goes missing, the ego will feel that a part of itself has been taken away. It will rant and rave while it stares longingly at the gap on the carpet where the stereo once stood.

Alternatively, you could understand and accept that the stereo is not really part of you. You can whistle your favorite tune and say to yourself, `Ah! I see they have come for the stereo!'

Often anger arises from losses that are not tangible. For example, the loss of importance or status, the loss of certainty, the loss of a familiar rhythm, the loss of opportunity, and a host of other possible or actual losses. As often as not, the anger generated is over the *possibility* of a loss rather than one that is actually suffered. Often the loss never materializes. It's the very thought of its possibility that drives you bonkers.

The answer is, don't attach too strongly to your possessions and the familiar circumstances of your life. If you do suffer a loss, just agree to suffer the loss. Usually, when things retreat from your life it seems traumatic initially but in the long term it is often very helpful. There is a deep spiritual process that keeps you cleansed and light and unencumbered. It is the very process that carries stuff away. Allow it. Thank it for granting you freedom—now you don't have to worry about someone pinching the stereo as you don't have one to worry about.

Once you have accepted the loss of whatever it is you've lost, you can, if you wish, set upon a course of action to retrieve the item or condition. But, before setting off, be sure the item is worth the effort of its retrieval. People become obsessed with their ego's view of justice. It creates prisons for them.

I chuckle over those stories of people who spend five years and half-a-million dollars going to court over some trivial issue; and finally the judge pronounces them right and awards them one dollar in damages. And the plaintiff struts to the front steps of the court house, all puffed up, silly as a mad goat, half-a-million poorer, pontificating about how they've been vindicated. Those twits get what they deserve, nothing. There is no percentage in being right, that's ego. The only percentage is in being free.

Don't allow anger to stay with you for long. It's very destructive. In a metaphysical sense, it's nuclear war. It is better to express your anger verbally than to internalize it silently. Long term, that can make you very sick. Better still, process your anger by scrutinizing the emotional flare you are experiencing. Get to the depth and meaning of it by searching for the loss.

In addition to the silent anger we sometimes feel, there is the theatrical anger people use to terrify and manipulate others into a prescribed course of action. The anger is not real. It is pretence, designed to cause the appropriate effect. You should not adopt the technique as it shows you up as manipulative and phony. When others use it against you, often it's hard to call their bluff—they will swear black and blue that their feigned reaction is real. They can't admit that some, or all, of their reaction is staged for the politics of the moment and for the benefit of their audience.

The human personality is often covert and dishonest. It's adept at maneuvering situations and people to its advantage.

It's a rare character who doesn't have any issues to defend, or hidden agenda they are trying to satisfy. It's even more rare to find someone who tells you openly what they feel or want. To cover their real intention, which may shift moment to moment, people lie or use half-truths. They try to obscure the real issue with red herrings; or use emotion to validate a dishonest or dubious position.

So someone might say, `I am very angry. You have really hurt my feelings.' Usually what they mean is, `I perceive you might or you have actually caused me some kind of loss. I can't allow you to set a precedent. Contradictions are an affront to my ego's sense of self. By blaming you for hurting my feelings, I am hoping to manipulate you into either backing off in the current situation or at least promising to toe the line in the future. By using theatrical anger and referring to my feelings, I can elevate my position in this issue to a greater importance than your side of the issue.'

The correct response is to tell the person that you've understood what they are saying—and then walk away, saying nothing more. If you feel it best to discuss the issue with them, take a line similar to this: 'I understand you when you say you feel hurt and angry, but I don't understand why you think I should be responsible for your reactions. In order for me to better understand your position, why don't you explain to me what it is you feel you've lost.'

Realization

Once you see that most anger is just a theatrical routine, you can diminish it to the irrelevance it deserves. All anger comes from loss. All loss is a security issue. All security issues are various manifestations of ego. Understand that and most anger becomes unnecessary.

9

Elevating Your Spirit

Chapter Nine

The way to eliminate the weight or anguish of your life quickly is to begin to discipline and control the ego. There is no emotional pain that is not ego-driven. We don't want to eliminate the ego completely. Otherwise we'd be wandering around the house each morning, drinking coffee for hours, saying 'Who the hell am I?'. We need the ego to sustain a sense of identity.

However, if you'll start by calling ego's bluff, and understanding the games it gets you into, you can develop strategies for managing things better. You really don't need any qualification or high-powered university degree to understand the psychology of the ego's machinations. Its ways are predictable and easy to understand.

Watch when it suckers you into importance. Stifle it when it seeks more and more gratification. Ignore it when it offers a hundred questions. Answer most of it's questions - let it know that you're not interested and that you just don't care.

When you experience frustration, look for the vision that's denied. Look at the time frames you've invested that vision with. Develop patience. If you see yourself as an infinite being, you have all eternity. You can wait forever if needs be.

When angry, look for the loss. When

you're sad, also look for the loss—sadness is just another manifestation of the same reaction. It's OK to be sad sometimes. Just agree to whatever loss is making you sad, then look for freshness and beauty and the life force. Happiness returns in a moment.

Remember, all mental weight comes from the interaction of two or more opposing forces in your mind—your reaction to circumstance, and your opinion or desire. You can fix most of the contradictions by controlling circumstances better and learning not to react when they don't suit. If you have less resistance, your opinions and desires will be less rigid. You'll learn to flow through life rather than fight your way along.

Learning to accept the contradictions of life is just a flip of the mind. Train your mind to be less dogmatic by offering it lots of self-imposed contradictions. Throw yourself into the icy lake of realism, don't let the ego play that cozy, safe, guaranteed game with you. You should never forget that your guarantee in life lies in the fact that you have none. That should spur you to action. Ignore the guarantee, get on with the journey. In the end, your energy—your perception and your ability—is all you have. Raise your energy and there's your guarantee. Discipline yourself and don't let little emotional upsets become large theatrical self-indulgences which destroy your stability and last *ages*. Change all the things you can easily change, accept most of the ones you can't change, and walk away from the rest.

Change your opinions, control the ego, and the light of spirit flows naturally from within your serenity. The more level and equitable your life becomes, the more the inner light of God shines through your mind—bypassing the ego and showing you a beauty and perception of life that most never even seek, let alone attain.

The light is always there, just beyond the veil of the brain's oscillations and the world of opinion, intellect and rigidity. One glimpse is enough. No words can properly describe the magnificence of the incandescent light of God. For within it is the very breath of life itself, and from it flows not just an overwhelming sense of love and security, but a sacred knowledge that beckons to us to reach beyond all earthly terms. Laced within that heavenly light is a glow, tempered in a diaphanous hue, the softness of which flows upon you more tenderly than the softest touch possible. It is through this softness that the human heart is settled. All anguish and fear is gently dispersed in the rapture of such a goodness, the like of which can only overwhelm the human mind in awe.

Dominate the ego, call the spirit forward in as much humility and poise as you can muster, and let that be your guide and your healer. Let the grace of it sweep through your life.

Yes. And imagine this ofttimes weary and frightened heart—all fear melted away, all anguish receding in the ghost of time. Yes, and see that same heart—fragile in its beauty, diligent in its task, beating quietly in the human breast, destined to eventual failure yet soldiering on in all circumstances—lovingly providing sustenance to the organism in silence.

Yes, and in that same heart, obligated and labored as it is by its chore, there is space for even more expansion and further obligation. It yearns and seeks and begs to be given it.

What obligation, we ask?

The obligation to carry a spark of the God force within itself. Not just for the benefit of the organism to which it is indentured, but to shine—ever so faintly perhaps, but shine all the while—for the benefit of others. So all shall see and remember, lest the reason for everything be forgotten in the turmoil of ego and spite, importance and power.

Yes, and if we listen quietly we will hear the heart as it calls from its hidden place saying, `Give me the light to carry, honor me with the obligation. Let me be the beast of burden and offer the enormity of that incandescence to my brothers and sisters. Let me shine to quiet the fears of our people, elevating and inspiring them, invigorating them in momentary glimpses of the heavenly light and a better world.'

Yes. And that heavenly light, beckoning all the while, yet never insisting. Silently reminding each to glimpse beyond sorrow and pain, beyond the illusion of our insecurity, to glimpse no less into the very depth of God's embrace.

Such is the wonder of it, no mortal can be but engulfed by its majesty. The nobility of which, flowing as a stream of light— sometimes gold, sometimes violet—passes through the human heart, silencing the mind, engulfing the emotions in a profound sensation. Pure love. Eternal love.

The quiet heart—so sweet and kind and full of compassion— reaches back within, seeking to find for itself a place to rest within that violet light of eternity. That humble wish, its grace, its simplicity, when granted is like a gentle kiss—the goodness of which tumbles upon you with the softness of a snowflake you imagine has fallen from the very hand of God.

Yes, and think again, what is life if not just a collection of experiences? And what are you if not just a memory of your reaction to those experiences? Better therefore to remember it well, proud and heroic. Put aside the silly foibles of the ego that tarnish the memory of you.

Accept and rejoice that such a great gift as this was bestowed by God personally, upon you. The gift of Life.

Accept the spirit within and let it heal you. Then walk through the lives of your people, teaching them the same process. And one day, some day, you may look back at your planet from a great place and you may smile. For you'll see the goodness of it all, gently spreading eon by eon to cover all of our people. And you'll remember that you were there in the early days, when the renaissance of that goodness was first launched.

`Yes,' you'll say, `I remember my life, I remember it well.

`It was most fine.'

We hope you enjoyed this Hay House book. If you would like to receive a free catalog featuring additional Hay House books and products, or if you would like information about the Hay Foundation, please write to:

Hay House, Inc.
1154 E. Dominguez St.
P.O. Box 6204
Carson, CA 90749-6204
(800) 654-5126

STUART WILDE International Tour and Seminar Information:

For information on Stuart Wilde's latest tour and seminar dates in the USA and Canada, contact:

White Dove International
P.O. Box 1000
Taos, NM 87571
(505) 758-0500—phone
(505) 758-2265—fax